Wildpeace

Not the peace of a cease-fire,
not even the vision of the wolf and the lamb,
but rather
as in the heart when the excitement is over
and you can talk only about a great weariness.
I know that I know how to kill,
that makes me an adult.
And my son plays with a toy gun that knows
how to open and close its eyes and say Mama.
A peace
without the big noise of beating swords into ploughshares,
without words, without
the thud of the heavy rubber stamp: let it be
light, floating, like lazy white foam.
A little rest for the wounds —
who speaks of healing?
(And the howl of the orphans is passed from one generation
to the next, as in a relay race:
the baton never falls.)

Let it come
like wildflowers,
suddenly, because the field
must have it: wildpeace.

Yehuda Amichai

Dedication

To the healers of history:
to those great and small,
daring and cautious,
brave and reluctant,
unrestrained and shy
— and every position
in between.

To those called
to speak into the
ancient dreamings
and the weepings
and the wounds
still seeping,
and remake them
according to the
pattern He unfolds
from heaven.

And to my mum,
who topped the state
in her high school geography exams
over seventy years ago.
Her sense of 'where'
and my sense of 'why'
have shaped the bookscape
you have in your hands.

Contents

1	*Wildpeace*
5	Introduction
6	*Shechem*
8	**The Return of the King**
16	Notes about the healing of Shechem's history
17	Comments about the healing of Shechem's history
18	Prayer
21	Discussion Questions
22	*Gadara*
25	**A Day in the Life**
38	Comments about the healing of Gadara's history
40	Notes about the healing of Gadara's history
41	Prayer
42	Discussion Questions
44	*Galilee*
47	**In Small Letters**
58	Comments about the healing of the Galilee's history
62	Prayer
63	Discussion Questions
65	*Pied Beauty*
66	Afterword
67	Acknowledgments and Attributions

Introduction

I was chatting over coffee with a friend of mine who is also a pastor. He asked me what projects I had planned for the coming year. I told him I was working on a book about Jesus healing history and the exquisite surprises of time and place involved.

He became animated with delight, and his eyes shone as I described some of the stories. 'A Christological theology of healing the land!' he exclaimed.

'You're way too excited about this,' I said. 'Why?'

'Oh, everyone does Paul,' he said. 'No one has looked at the theological aspects of Jesus healing the land.'

'I'm thinking art and story more than theology,' I said.

'I know you,' he retorted. 'You won't be able to help yourself. The stories will be spilling over with theology.'

It seems he was right. Each section in this book starts with a short narrative work — a gospel story retold from the viewpoint of an eyewitness. Although I have added some commentary after each narrative, I wanted this presentation to be less about information and more about immersion into first century Jewish culture. I want you to *be there*, and hope you will see with your heart, not just your mind.

After a downpour of rain on my lawn, storm lilies often spring up — pale, delicate, tinged with lilac. Their appearance is sudden, unexpected, because even though I've watered those same spots, the lilies seem to know it wasn't a cloudburst from heaven.

Like Wildflowers, Suddenly is named for this rain-prompted appearance of beauty in the landscape. When Jesus brought a grace-drenched healing to a person, He tailored His restoration so that it also wrought healing in the land and in history itself. In some cases, He also reclaimed honour for God. When, by word or action, He took back the names of God that had been stolen by enemy principalities, He was reclaiming the soul of the nation.

May God be honoured and grace bloom for you as you read.

.

Anne Hamilton

Seventeen Mile Rocks, 2019

It is to you that I am giving Shechem,
that fertile region which I took from the Amorites
with my sword and my bow.

Genesis 48:22 GNT

John 4:5 BSB

So He came to a town of Samaria
called Sychar, near the plot of ground
Jacob had given his son Joseph.

Samaritans worshipping on Mt Gerizim

The Return of the King

A narrative retelling of the healing of Shechem from the perspective of the woman of Samaria.

Barefoot, the woman wended her way down the ancient path. Her water-pot was on her shoulder, her steps cautious, her eyes wary. Her gaze drifted to the south, to the hill of green Gerizim. A lone shepherd, tiny with distance, moved with his flock across slopes flecked with red anemone flowers. A hot wind scattered their petals to the sky, staining the blue with droplets of blood.

As the path turned, the woman caught sight of Gerizim's northern twin — bald Ebal. Its rocky heights seemed to slump in the heat.

It was about noon — the hour of safety. The woman was sure her neighbours would be avoiding the midday sun. And although pilgrims often stopped to pray and pay ancestral homage at the well in Sychar, they would be in town by now. She was confident they'd be swarming through Shechem, buying food and resting from the heat, not down by the well.

She skipped down the last few steps. By the time she reached the bottom and realised her mistake, it was too late to retreat without being noticed.

Because — there — hidden in the shadows of the gnarled terebinth tree was a solitary man.

A Jew, by the look of him.

She stared. His hand was resting against the pillar of witness, the standing stone Joshua had set up in ages past. Such presumption. *Should I tell to take his defilement elsewhere?*

She decided to ignore him. *Let's pretend we're both alone.* So she dropped her gaze and slid the pot from her shoulder.

Shechem, *ridge or shoulder*: the portion of land which Jacob bequeathed to his favourite son Joseph on his deathbed. Joseph wanted to be buried in his inheritance so left instructions his bones were to be taken from Egypt when the Israelites left.

Gerizim, *cut in two*: one of two mountains above the town of Shechem. Moses directed that six tribes of the people of Israel were to assemble here to pronounce covenant blessings.

Ebal, *bald or bare:* one of two mountains above the town of Shechem. Moses directed that six tribes of the people of Israel were to pronounce curses from this mountain during covenant re-affirmation.

Sychar, *drink, alcohol;* also overtones of *threshold, falsehood* and *wages:* the locality at Shechem where Jacob dug a well and buried his idols under a terebinth tree. His grandfather Abram built the first of seven altars here, also under a terebinth.

Terebinth, *pistacia palaestina,* a variety of tree common in Israel. In Hebrew, the word is 'elah' and is traditionally translated *oak*.

'Give me a drink.'

She blinked, stunned. *What are you saying, Jew?*

Then a surge of anger rose, unbidden. *Am I your servant, your cup-bearer?*

The thought ignited a torrent of flames in her mind. *Don't you know that there's a good reason Jewish men do not associate with Samaritan women? And that reason is the laws made by a priest and enforced by a cup-bearer?*

The injustices of history flared like a roaring firestorm. *Are you deliberately trying to provoke me? Understand this, Jew: the final rupture between our peoples was because of a cup-bearer!*

She took a deep breath as she watched him stroke the pillar of witness. Joshua's long-ago words, spoken at this very spot, echoed in her mind: 'Choose for yourselves who you will serve.'

Choose. Serve. The turmoil in her thoughts stilled. *It's time to get a few things straight.* 'You are a Jew and I am a Samaritan woman. How can you ask me for a drink?'

He ignored her blunt tone. His reply was soft, his voice edged with quiet serenity. 'If you knew the gift of God and who it is that asks you for a drink, you would have asked him and he would have given you living water.'

Living water? The woman touched her water-pot. *So you're not insulting me.* She frowned. *Because you are now offering to be MY cupbearer.* She dropped her eyes again, considering the words of this Jewish riddle-maker. *And if you were in fact alluding to Nehemiah the cupbearer before, you've just redeemed the snub.*

Living water? She pressed her lips together as she tried to recall the significance of living water for the Jews. *Is this instead about Rehoboam, your king of the line of David? The one who lost his kingdom? Right here on this spot, as a matter of fact. When he came here because of our living water.*

She raised her face, daring to look him intently, straight in the eyes. *Kingship? A reunited kingdom? Insane! Of course, if it wasn't insane, you're at the right place.*

Nehemiah, *God comforts*: the cupbearer to the Persian king Artaxerxes, who was opposed by the Samaritans when became a governor of Judah. He was supported by the priest Ezra who wanted to re-instate the Law, rebuild the Temple, and preserve racial purity.

Living water, one of the two most important ceremonial requirements for the installation of a king. The other was anointing oil.

Joshua, *God saves*, successor to Moses. He directed the conquest of the Promised Land and twice brought the people to Shechem to reaffirm the national covenant with God in the way Moses had left instructions.

His gaze was steady, his eyes full of twinkling delight. He didn't seem mad.

But... you can't possibly be suggesting you're a king! She took a deep breath. *And you want me — ME! — as your cupbearer?*

'Sir, you have nothing to draw with and the well is deep. Where can you get this living water? Are you greater than our father Jacob, who gave us the well and drank from it himself, as did also his sons and his livestock?' *Let's see what he does with that bait. If he's really claiming he's a king, he will admit to being greater than Jacob.*

'Everyone who drinks this water will be thirsty again, but whoever drinks the water I give them will never thirst. Indeed, the water I give them will become in them a spring of water welling up to eternal life.'

What? No.

The woman took a step back. *This is more than bringing back the kingship of the line of David! Vastly more than reuniting the kingdom.* She tried to marshal her thoughts. *He's saying he's the Lord's Messiah! What on earth would the Messiah be doing here?*

And then, as a frisson of understanding shivered up her spine, her hand flew to her mouth. *Oh, but of course, he HAS to come here!*

She looked towards Mount Ebal, the ridge of cursing, then to Mount Gerizim, the hill of blessing — and finally towards the town of Shechem nestling between the two. *Where else can the Messiah receive the government upon his shoulder?* Shechem was the logical place: here at Abraham's tree, Jacob's well, Joshua's stone, Joseph's tomb — all in the shadow of God's mountain.

The Jews might dispute that last statement about God's mountain. However, they did not dispute this land was the inheritance Jacob had bequeathed to Joseph on his deathbed. *Is that why you're here? To claim an inheritance as a son of Joseph? If you are the Messiah, then which one are you claiming to be — the kingly Messiah, David's son, or the war messiah, Joseph's son?*

The woman took a deep breath, then another. She turned her gaze to the twisted trunk of terebinth, allowing the weight of its history to calm her racing mind. Under this very tree, Abraham built his first

Messiah, *the anointed one.* In the time of Jesus, two Messiahs were expected — a king from the tribe of Judah who would be known as the 'Son of David' and a warrior from the tribe of Ephraim or Manasseh who would be called the 'Son of Joseph'. John's gospel always refers to Jesus as the 'Son of Joseph', never the 'Son of David', indicating his presentation of Jesus is to highlight his role as the war messiah.

Foreign women: the line of Jesus contains several women who were Gentiles — Tamar the Canaanite woman, Ruth from Moab, Rahab of Jericho. Some scholars consider that even Bathsheba, wife of David, was a Gentile. Joseph apparently married a Gentile — Asenath, the daughter of the Egyptian priest. Moses married Zipporah of Midian. Rebekah, wife of Isaac, was a Gentile too.

altar in this land and turned his back on the gods of his fathers. Under this very tree, Jacob dug this well and buried his household gods. Under this very tree, Joshua raised a stone and called for the people to throw away their foreign gods.

The history of this place is about renouncing other gods. *Ahhh... Am I being challenged to give up something? But I have nothing! Does he have any clue how hard my life has been?* 'Sir, give me this water so that I won't get thirsty and have to keep coming here to draw water.'

'Go, call your husband and come back.'

She froze. *Careful, careful, careful what you say, girl. Don't let the old wounds open again.* 'I have no husband.'

'You are right when you say you have no husband. The fact is, you have had five husbands, and the man you now have is not your husband. What you have just said is quite true.'

He knows! The woman realised the riddle-maker was not looking at her. *Or does he know?* His gaze was fixed on the tree. *Who is he speaking to — me or the land?*

Five husbands. Five covenants. Yes, here our ancestors re-affirmed covenant five times. Here Abraham chose God, Jacob chose God,

Abimelech, *my father is king*, the son of Gideon. He killed seventy of his brothers on a single stone and was proclaimed king beside the terebinth at the pillar in Shechem. He was the first king *in* Israel, though not *of* Israel.

Joseph chose God, Joshua chose God — and there was an evil choosing too, under Gideon's son, Abimelech.

Here Abimelech became the first king in Israel. And here the kingship was ripped away from Rehoboam. *We're back to kings. And, if he's talking to the land, does he mean that it chose not to have a husband when our ancestors rejected Rehoboam? Is he telling us to go back to Zion?* 'Sir, I can see that you are a prophet. Our ancestors worshipped on this mountain, but you Jews claim that the place where we must worship is in Jerusalem.'

'Woman, believe me, a time is coming when you will worship the Father neither on this mountain nor in Jerusalem.'

Neither? She shook her head ever so slightly, unsure she'd heard correctly.

'You Samaritans worship what you do not know; we worship what we do know, for salvation is from the Jews. Yet a time is coming and has now come when the true worshippers will worship the Father in the Spirit and in truth, for they are the kind of worshippers the Father seeks. God is spirit, and his worshippers must worship in the Spirit and in truth.'

In Spirit and truth? Has now *come? Right* now*? Stop your teasing, riddle-maker — time to be direct and speak to the point.* 'I know that Messiah is coming. When he comes, he will explain everything to us.'

His gaze came down from the tree to rest on her. His hand left the pillar of witness to gesture in blessing. 'I, the one speaking to you — I am he.'

Rehoboam, *nation is enlarged*, the son of Solomon and grandson of David. He came to Shechem to be anointed king. His arrogance caused a permanent rupture in the kingdom — two tribes remaining loyal to the line of David and forming the Kingdom of Judah while the other ten tribes split off to form the apostate Kingdom of Israel.

Samaria, *watchtower*, a hill brought by Omri, the sixth king of Israel, as the site for his capital. About forty kilometres north-west of Shechem, it eventually gave its name to the people of the northern kingdom.

Her heart skipped a beat. *Does it matter which Messiah? The son of David or the son of Joseph?* The woman felt a slow-spreading smile begin to curve across her lips.

The riddle-maker's companions arrived in a sudden bustle of noise. A startled silence fell as they realised they were interrupting a conversation. But there was nothing more she needed to know.

The king had returned. She was called as his cup-bearer; she was called too as his herald. Five times married, she was called to represent the land with its five covenants. After a thousand years, the king had come to re-unify the kingdom. He had come to heal history… and her wounded heart.

She didn't yet know his name but she knew he'd come to restore her. As well as the land.

Choose, Joshua had said. So she did. She left her water-pot to hurry back to Sychar and spread the unbelievably good news.

Son of David and Son of Joseph: two Messiahs were anticipated in the time of Jesus — a kingly Messiah as well as a war Messiah. The kingly Messiah would come from the tribe of Judah and the line of David; while the war Messiah was expected to come from the tribe of Joseph. Matthew, Mark and Luke all emphasise Jesus as the 'son of David' while John exclusively uses the term 'son of Joseph'.

God is spirit, and those who worship Him must worship in spirit and truth.

John 4:24 WEB

Notes:

Samaritans means *guardians, keepers, watchers*. After the invasion of the northern Kingdom by the Assyrians, Samaria was defeated and much of the populace taken captive. The area was soon repopulated under Assyrian policy by the peoples of other conquered nations. As a result of racial mix due to intermarriage, the Samaritans who were left were no longer considered genuine descendants of Abraham through Isaac and Jacob. The issue of purity came to a head under the leadership of Ezra and Nehemiah when those Jewish men who had married foreign wives were pressured to divorce them, even when children were involved.

Comments:

The story of Jesus appointing a woman as His 'first' evangelist is so well-known that it needs little introduction. Yet it's difficult to locate the incident within the timeframe of Jesus' ministry. Only John writes of it and, while it would seem to be an early event from its placement within his gospel, there are no specific calendar clues to enable us to date it with any real certainty. In fact, since John's account of Jesus is constructed in mirrored scenes, its positioning seems to have been mainly determined by its literary pairing with Jesus' trial before Pilate.

'What on earth,' you may wonder, 'does the story of the Samaritan woman have in common with Pilate's questioning of Jesus?' Yet, look closer and there you'll see the same themes:

- the nature of truth,
- a choice about kingship,
- decisions about covenant and government,
- the use of water.

There are old, strong echoes in the fine detail of this story for readers acquainted with the history of Shechem. It is no coincidence that Jesus goes there, meets a five-times-married woman, and works their conversation with around to the topics of living water and anointing. If you're going to heal history, you need someone to perfectly represent the history of the land. And a five-times-married woman fits the bill for a location where five covenant ratifications took place.

Jesus had a deliberate agenda in going to Shechem. The first king in Israel was proclaimed at this place, and so He wanted the proclamation of the last king to happen there too. That's what is behind the fact that '*He had to go through Samaria.*' Despite what it says in John 4:4, He didn't really *have* to go that way at all. There were other routes — longer, yes; more time-consuming, definitely — but it wasn't the only road from Jerusalem to Galilee.

The only reason He *had* to go there was because He had a divine appointment — under a tree, by a well, next to a standing stone. There He put a train of events in motion, trusting the Samaritans would proclaim Him as the Messiah. Such an announcement would heal the breach caused by Rehoboam's defiant arrogance and re-unify the ancient kingdoms of Judah and Israel under a single head. The kingship would finally return to the line of David.

When — later — Pilate too acknowledges Him as a king, He has achieved His goal: as the declared sovereign of the Jews, the Samaritans and Gentiles, He can save the world.

'For to us a child is born, to us a son is given, and the government will be on his shoulders,' said the prophet Isaiah. *Shoulders* were a symbol of *government* for the Hebrew people — because authority was conferred or transferred in those times by placing keys upon another person's shoulder. Because Shechem meant *shoulder*, it symbolised a place where government was authorised. It was a natural place to ratify covenants.

Everything Jesus did at Jacob's Well was carefully and prayerfully pre-meditated to bring down the dividing wall between the Jews and the Samaritans. To usher in the Kingdom and call forth peace. *'He is our peace,'* Paul wrote to the Ephesians.

The terrible division caused by the actions of Ezra the priest and Nehemiah, cupbearer to the Persian king, when they sent the foreign women away, began to be healed by the simplest of actions: asking for a drink. With no more fanfare than that, Jesus began to heal history.

You know, you too are called to heal history, to mend the world, to bind up the broken-hearted, to call forth peace.

So how will you choose to do that today? As Jesus demonstrates, perhaps it's as simple as a drink: a bottle of water or a cup of coffee. Or perhaps it's a little larger in scope: sponsoring a water project or the building of a well. Whatever it is, prayerfully and carefully allow God to set the agenda so that His Kingdom and His glory will be revealed.

We are steeped in tradition. We don't know it and we delude ourselves into thinking we are different from what we really are. But the memory of all the trauma that has affected our generational lines remains in our genes and shapes us and our decision-making. We are so very like the Samaritan woman: suspicious of strangers, separated from our neighbours, wounded by relationships, surrounded by symbols of God's faithfulness yet living with the pain of history.

Prayer:

Come, Lord Jesus — You alone have the power to mend the world. I pray you start with me. I am like the woman at Jacob's Well — I need Your healing touch. I am surrounded by ancestral iniquity but it's so familiar I am unaware of its nature. I confess I am suspicious of those I don't know. I question their motives. I think I know better than others and believe they must be wrong.

I admit too to the irony of being proud of my humility. I am sorry. Forgive me, Lord.

Father, give me true humility — and a contrite heart. Cleanse my family lines through the power of the blood of Jesus. Re-mould me and re-make me so I am a true herald in Your unified kingdom. Heal my brokenness and give me the awareness there are no strangers — only friends I haven't yet met. But at the same time gift me with Your discernment, Lord, as to whom I can trust.

Father, You sent Jesus to heal the history of the land just as much as You sent Him to heal our personal history. Your friend at Jacob's Well lived at Shechem — an area desperate for deep healing. It had been ripped apart by trauma and violence for over 1700 years. But Lord, this too is the story of my own life and land. Send Jesus, Lord, to us.

Lord, I've used anger to get my own way. I repent of the pain this caused others. Many times I withdrew and isolated in response to other people's outbursts — thus creating an icy impenetrable wall between us. This was just as sinful and out of alignment with You as anger was. I am sorry, Lord. I thought I was protecting myself but this is not Your way. Forgive me, Father. I am sorry and repent for the many times I responded to pride and manipulation with equally strong pride and manipulation, thus accelerating a war of words and violence. Forgive me, Lord. This is not Your way, either.

Father, teach me Your ways. Be my Guide.

Lord, our land has been ravaged by greed and selfishness. We have not acknowledged You as Creator and Sustainer. We have exploited the land for profit without considering the long-term effects. We have overstocked with livestock, over-planted crops, destroyed irreplaceable forests and failed to recognise that wasting the earth's bounty is despising Your precious gifts to us. We ignore the need of the earth to refresh and renew just like we do. You observed a Sabbath rest and commanded that we and the land do similarly.

We have been negligent, Lord, and are sorry. Open our eyes to Your beauty all around us. We know Your laws but we fail to honour them. Forgive us for our lack of stewardship. Heal us and heal the earth we have ravished. Show us how to mend the world as Jesus did.

In His mighty name. Amen.

Discussion Questions:

(1) The meeting between Jesus and the woman at the well is reminiscent of the stories of the patriarchs who met their wives by a well: Moses and Zipporah; Jacob and Rachel; Eliezer, representing Isaac, and Rebekah. Is there any significance to the meeting place with regard to the Bride of Christ?

(2) Who was the town of Shechem named after? (See Genesis 34) What happened to him and why? Discuss the possibility that Jesus is also healing this aspect of history as well.

(3) According to Acts 7:16, who is buried at Shechem? How might this have impacted Rehoboam's decision to be crowned there, rather than at Jerusalem? What aspects of Shechem's name and history play into its standing as a symbol of government?

(1) What is a herald? Are you called to this role in the Kingdom?

(2) What is a cupbearer? Are you called to this role in the Kingdom?

Gadara

Blessed be he who enlarges Gad!
Gad crouches like a lion; he tears off arm and scalp.

— Deuteronomy 33:20 ESV —

— Matthew 8:28 NLT —

When Jesus arrived in the region of the Gadarenes,
two men who were possessed by demons met Him.
They were so violent no one could go through that area.

A Day in the Life

A narrative retelling of the healing of Gadara from the viewpoint of the apostle Matthew.

I thought everyone knew the story. It's so famous I thought the whole world grew up with it. Oh, fair enough, pardon the slight exaggeration, perhaps not the *entire* world.

The blue-painted tribes from the wilds of Caledonia obviously missed out on hearing about it. Maybe a few of their bards or druids knew but, honestly, I just can't see any of them uttering any Roman general's name aloud these days. Except maybe in a curse. And, true enough, at the other end of the empire there's no doubt the horse-mad Parthian hordes don't use the story as part of their training curriculum either.

Still, everyone in the civilised world — everywhere the Pax Romana, *the peace of Rome,* rules — has heard the tale. To me, it's unimaginable that anyone educated in any school anywhere hasn't heard some version of it. It doesn't matter if the school is an elite private academy supervised by a hand-picked Greek tutor or if it's an undisciplined rabble shepherded by a rustic rabbi in a remote synagogue. Everyone knows about Julius Caesar and the storm.

But I'm guessing it's news to you. So let me back up and add some explanatory detail to my account of the day.

To begin with, let me say that it was a gruelling experience. I was absolutely exhausted, and all I was doing was scribbling down notes. I can't imagine how drained Jesus felt. We were high up a mountain looking down on the placid lake — half-way between heaven and earth, it seemed — on one of those flat grassy areas that make it easy for people to gather and listen. The weather was perfect: honey-warm sunshine, a light wind riffling the clumps of narcissus and rock rose.

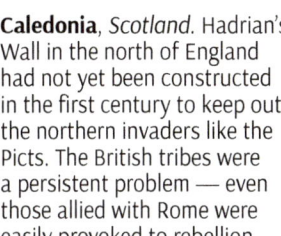

Caledonia, *Scotland*. Hadrian's Wall in the north of England had not yet been constructed in the first century to keep out the northern invaders like the Picts. The British tribes were a persistent problem — even those allied with Rome were easily provoked to rebellion.

Parthians, *the ancient people of modern day Iran*. The eastern limit of the Roman empire changed many times. The towns and cities of Trans-jordan were just behind the frontier zone known as the 'limes' which was protected from the Parthians by a series of forts.

Jesus had everyone's attention and, for once, He used it to teach. He gave us all a long, extended download from heaven, spiced with several dashes of controversy. I'm sure you've heard of the lecture. Parts of it have become immeasurably famous for flying in the face of established convention. You know: the love-your-enemies bit, the looking-lustfully-equals-adultery bit, the do-unto-others-as-you-would-have-them-do-unto-you bit, the don't-let-your-right-hand-know-what-your-left-hand-is-doing-when-it-comes-to-generosity bit.

As the day drew on, people came and went up and down the mountain. Some brought food for their friends, some brought more of their friends. A messenger came for Peter, bringing troubling news. His wife's mother had a deadly fever. He didn't say anything to Jesus at first because he never dreamed the talk would go on so long. But by late afternoon, Peter was quietly getting anxious and agitated. He really wanted Jesus to get a move on and start heading down the mountain. But even when Jesus finally finished the lecture and set off for Capernaum, it wasn't simple to get away.

Hebrew glossary:

Rose (as in *rose* of Sharon): *habasselet* meaning *overshadowed by God's love*.

Now the talk was over, it seemed the crowd had taken that as a signal for a healing session to begin. A man was waiting beside the track on the way down, right in the middle of a circle of meadow flowers — narcissus and crocus — rattling his bells. Perhaps you know the name of these blossoms in the old language? Solomon called them *habasselet*, 'overshadowed by divine love'.

The man with leprosy didn't even need to shout 'Unclean, unclean' to get Jesus' attention. He knelt down and said, 'Lord, if You are willing, You can make me clean.' Jesus went to Him, and affirmed him — lingering as He often did to heal heart and soul as well as skin.

By this stage, of course, Peter was really trying to curb his impatience. A good thing as it turned out. Because eventually, when Jesus was on His way again, He'd no sooner got to the gates of Capernaum than a centurion bailed Him up. Yes, a Roman no less — and waiting expressly for Him.

Centurion: an officer in a Roman legion in charge of one hundred troops.

It surprised us. First, that the Romans were paying attention to Jesus and taking Him seriously. Second, that Jesus took him seriously back. *Too* seriously, in lots of people's minds. Anyway, this soldier had a request about his servant and Jesus, as He always did, responded to the smallest measure of faith.

Let me describe for you exactly what happened because it sets the tone for the rest of the day's events.

'Lord,' he said, 'my servant lies at home paralysed, suffering terribly.'

Jesus said to him, 'Shall I come and heal him?'

The centurion replied, 'Lord, I do not deserve to have You come under my roof. But just say the word, and my servant will be healed. For I myself am a man under authority, with soldiers under me. I tell this one, "Go," and he goes; and that one, "Come," and he comes. I say to my servant, "Do this," and he does it.'

When Jesus heard this, he was amazed and said to those following Him, 'Truly I tell you, I have not found anyone in Israel with such great faith.'

Of all the nuances in the conversation — and there are too many to explore here — there's one that characterised everything from that moment on. Did you catch it? It was the *nature of authority*.

Well, Jesus of course granted the centurion's request, and then — finally — headed off to heal Peter's mother-in-law. That done, she got up and fixed a bite to eat for Him and the rest of us. I think she was a bit flustered at all the attention. Anyway, it was a lovely finale to a glorious day — is that what you're thinking? Time for a well-earned rest. All done and dusted with that one last domestic miracle.

Not at all. Word had got around.

When evening came, a whole crowd of demon-possessed people rocked up for healing. That wasn't all. Another crowd of sick people came for healing as well. And that wasn't all either. Yet another crowd — curiosity-seekers, I guess — turned up too. I just wanted to escape. I think we all did. Even Jesus — ever-patient, ever-uncomplaining Jesus — had had enough. He told Peter and the rest of us to get a boat ready to go to the other side of the lake.

Let me tell you it isn't easy to make a run for it with hundreds of people watching your every move and ready to follow you wherever you go. But — another miracle to add to the tally — somehow we managed it. We got Jesus away from the crowd and slipped Him undercover on board the boat. Not unnaturally, given the day He'd had, He was asleep the moment He put His head on the bench.

Luke: the Greek doctor who authored a gospel and the book of Acts

Dio Cassius: a Roman statesman and historian who wrote 80 volumes of history.

Plutarch: Greek biographer and essayist

Appian: Greek historian

Suetonius: Roman historian and biographer of the equestrian order

Florus: Roman historian and possibly poet

Lucan: a Roman poet

Then we pushed off the shore and headed into the darkness.

Right, now I guess this would be the best moment for a brief intermission.

Gerasa: also the region of Gergesa, *the place of fighting or pilgrimage,* in the land of the Gadarenes which was situated on the eastern shore of the Sea of Galilee

Just to inform you about Julius Caesar and the storm. I don't know how you could have missed out learning about such a famous episode. What on earth do schools teach these days? Why, Dio Cassius, Plutarch, Appian, Suetonius, Florus and Lucan — just to name a few of the more well-known ones — all re-tell the story in their various embellished ways. Most people are sure it's history, not legend — simply because it doesn't exactly reflect well on his high-and-mightiness. Nobody expects humility from Caesar or any of his successors — let's face it, they're in a position to dish out as much pride, arrogance and egotism as they like.

But... well, I won't draw the moral out. I'll let you judge for yourself. Stripped of all its florid exaggeration, the story goes like this: Julius Caesar, needing to find out why his troops were delayed in arriving at the front, disguised himself as a slave and went aboard a twelve-oared boat. A storm blew up as the vessel attempted to pass over a

Most High God: *El Elyon* in Deuteronomy 32:8 where the distribution of the nations is described.

river bar into the sea. The cross-currents were so dangerous that the captain decided to turn back before they all drowned. At the moment he gave this order, Caesar threw off his disguise and declared, 'Be of good courage, men, knowing you carry Caesar and Caesar's fortune.'

Remember the *nature of authority*? Yes, it's true that Caesar might have had supreme military authority over all the legions of a massive army. However, he didn't have a jot or a tittle over wind or wave. So, despite the redoubled vigour of the rowers and their most strenuous efforts on his behalf, the boat was forced to retreat. And Caesar, as you might guess, was mightily displeased.

Consider again: the nature of *authority*. And make sure that, onto the mental hook where you've hung this word *authority*, you add another two words from this story about the illustrious Julius: *troops* and *fortune*.

End of digression. Intermission over.

So back to Jesus, sleeping on the boat. And us, starting to panic. Well, me starting to panic, if truth be told. A savage storm had swept in without warning and water was crashing in foaming cascades over the sides of the vessel. In my former line of work — that'd be tax-collecting, in case you haven't realised — I hardly need tell you that going out in boats on lakes in the middle of the night was simply never called for. It was only when Peter, Andrew, James and John who actually *had* made a habit of going out in boats on lakes in the middle of the night in their former line of work — that'd be fishing — all started looking white and worried, that I started wanting to bail out. Both the water and myself.

Little-faiths: Dallas Willard in *The Divine Conspiracy* suggests Jesus made up this word Himself.

I don't know who shook Jesus awake. I know I wanted to. He didn't even sound exasperated when He responded to our desperate fear of drowning. 'Little-faiths,' He chided. 'Why are you so afraid?' Then He rebuked the wind and the waves — and, instantly, there was silence.

Except for our gasps. 'What kind of man is this? Even the winds and the waves obey Him.'

None of us were brave enough to say it but we were all thinking: *so, Julius Caesar, the lord of the legions couldn't come anywhere near this. It follows that someone far greater than the lord of the legions is here.*

The moment felt like the culmination of the entire day. But little did we know: it was just a prelude. Merely an itty-bitty warm-up.

When we got to the other side of the lake, we were too tired to turn back. The wind had blown us down to the territory of the Gadarenes so we thought we'd just head up to Gadara or Gerasa and get some supplies. In ancient times, before the division of the land into the Kingdoms of Judah and Israel, this territory had been the allotment of land given to the tribe of Gad. These days, however, it was Gentile territory. Not precisely and exactly the eastern border with the Parthians, but close. The local towns were basically staging-grounds just behind the frontier. They supplied the string of forts at the limits of empire. So, as you might suspect, Roman legions were marching through these places every other day of the week.

Like I said: this was the ancient homeland of the tribe of Gad, one of the twelve sons of our forefather Jacob. Now Gad is a name with two meanings. It does double duty as a wonderful pun: *fortune* and *troop*. If your mind has flitted back to Julius Caesar saying, 'Be of good courage, men, knowing you carry Caesar and Caesar's fortune,' and if you're finding further echoes of his story continuing on as we disembarked our boat, you'd be right on target. Maybe you're getting the significance of the legions criss-crossing this landscape too.

We were heading up towards town when out of some caves came a couple of naked men, rattling chains, and screaming at the top of their lungs as if they were demon-possessed. Turns out the reason is because they actually *are* demon-possessed.

And they've got an interesting take on who Jesus is. They identified Him as the son of the Most High God and asked if He's come to torment them. Now it dawned on me at the time that title they were making free with was really intriguing. 'Most High God' isn't just any random pick from Scripture: it's the particular name of Yahweh when talking about Him as the One who made the allotment for the nations. And there we were — in what was basically a Gentile nation: yet they were acknowledging the authority of God. That was a turn-up: the Gentiles, acknowledging the supremacy of our God. It first occurs when Melchizedek is introduced in the Book of Beginnings and he blesses Abram in the name of El Elyon.

Now up to this point, I'd been under an illusion. I thought I'd been terrified out of my mind during the storm on the lake. But — as these

Demons: understood in the time of Jesus to be the disembodied spirits of the deceased giants born to the angelic *bene elohim*, sons of God, who mated with human women. The giants were the nephilim and their spirits continually seek an invitation to inhabit a human or animal host.

monstrously strong madmen charged towards us, I suddenly realised I was grossly mistaken. I was looking around wildly for a safe place to run to when, just as Jesus calmed the storm, He calmed these two men. At this point I'd like to borrow a tiny extra detail from the account of this same incident by my good friend, Doctor Luke. Jesus asked one of the men his name but it was the demon who answered: 'Legion,' it said, 'for we are many.'

Legion.

Now I hope you can see how events had been building up to this very moment. It started with a centurion, a legionnaire, acknowledging the authority of Jesus. It continued with the wind and the waves acknowledging His authority too. Did they blow across the lake and proclaim to the farthest shore, 'He's coming. He's coming. The One who is greater than the lord of the legions is on His way'?

When I remember that morning, I hear something else in the voice of the wind — something that I'm sure I didn't actually notice at the time but nevertheless is strangely vivid in my memory when I think back on all that happened. 'Render to Caesar the things that are Caesar's,' the wind whispered, 'and to Him the things that are His.'

Well, I'm sure you know what occurred next. Jesus healed the men and allowed the demons to enter some pigs. I wouldn't have thought it, but it turns out there are just some things a pig won't do. And hosting the shades of the nephilim is apparently one of them. So, off the pigs dashed, heading straight for the nearest water to neutralise the demons. They were pursued by a couple of shocked and shouting swineherds who tried to arrest their flight. But to no avail. They plunged off a cliff in their panic — and there they drowned.

All of which meant that, as soon as the story got out, we were most definitely unwelcome in Gerasa. In fact, the end result was that, although Jesus cast the demons out of the two men as well as out of the landscape, He was in turn Himself cast out of the city.

I suppose we should have seen it as prophetic of what was to come. But we missed all the signs, all the clues. We were so full of wonderment at His authority over disease and weather and demons that it seemed like a trifling inconvenience on the way to bigger and better things.

Water as a means of neutralising demons: the long-held tradition that witches do not like water, that evil spirits cannot cross running water and that the shades of the nephilim are neutralised by the waters of baptism is derived from first century Jewish understanding which can be found alluded to in 2 Peter 2:4–10 in combination with 1 Peter 3:19–21.

Only long after He was finally killed in Jerusalem, an outcast condemned to die on the cross beyond the outer gate, did we finally begin to see the hints that had always been there.

Only then too did we start to understand that He didn't start healing the land and its history after He rose from the dead. It was something He did wherever He went.

Comments:

The story of the stilling of the storm has many evocative allusions. I have chosen to tell the story above through the eyes of Matthew who collected taxes for the Romans, because his slant on it would no doubt have been different from that of someone like Peter or his brother Andrew, the sons of the fisherman Jonah. They — almost certainly — would have thought of their father's namesake, the prophet Jonah who came from Gath-hepher in Galilee. (2 Kings 14:25) As an aside, let's note this means that, when the Pharisees were seeking to denigrate Jesus by insisting that no prophet had ever come from Galilee (John 7:52), they were quite wrong.

Jonah's flight from God's calling on his life — to proclaim repentance to the Assyrians of Nineveh — put the lives of an entire ship's crew at risk. Like Jesus, he was asleep when a violent storm blew up. Like Jesus, he was woken by his very frightened travelling companions who thought they were about to die.

Jonah, however, knew that his rebellion was the cause of the raging tempest and suggested that the sailors throw him overboard. They were reluctant but eventually felt there was no other choice. And as soon as they did, the storm ceased.

So when Jesus said, 'Peace! Be still!' to the storm, perhaps these good Jewish boys thought back to the story of Jonah and realised, as Jesus Himself was to say at another time, 'And behold, greater than Jonah is here.' (Luke 11:32 BLB)

Still, let's remember that the Jewish people had lived under the direct yoke of the Romans for over six decades. They would have known the stories of the Latin heroes. They would have known the story of Julius Caesar attempting to calm a storm — and failing. I have little doubt that running through the minds of these disciples would also have been the thought: 'And behold, greater than Caesar is here.'

It might well have seemed to the disciples that their boat was driven ashore quite randomly. But just as Jesus *had* to go through Samaria, it seems to me Jesus *had* to go through a potentially fatal storm on His way to heal the land on the far side of the Sea of Galilee. The one thing He always wanted to activate healing was faith. So in two incidents He demonstrated His matchless authority. In doing so, He awakened a tiny shoot of faith in His disciples that He was greater than the most legendary Lord of the Legions who had ever dazzled the Roman world.

And that specific aspect of faith — relating to *authority*, *troops* and *fortune* — was what He wanted as He headed into the very territory where a man possessed by 'Legion' lived.

Like the woman at the well whose five marriages represented the five covenant ratifications of Shechem, the man also symbolised the land itself. And in healing him, Jesus also healed the 'land of the troops'.

Notes:

A friend of mine suffered for many years from a form of agoraphobia — fear of open spaces. He couldn't leave his home without risking a terrifying panic attack. Many times he asked members of his church's prayer team to come to his house and pray for him. But they always insisted he demonstrate his faith by coming to them instead. He made an interesting comment at one point: 'If I had a broken leg, the church wouldn't ask me to show my faith by coming to them. But because it's a mental illness, they see it differently.'

In the story of the healing of the demon-possessed men, we miss the fact it wasn't the faith of the men which counted. And it certainly wasn't the faith of the demons! Just as in the story of the paralysed man whose friends made a hole in the roof to lower him down in front of Jesus, it was the faith of the onlookers that counted.

And we don't need much faith. No more than a mustard seed's worth. Just enough to hold on to the hem of Jesus' garment — His prayer shawl — because, in reality, it's not our faith that counts in the final analysis. It's His faith and His prayer before the Father that changes everything — both for us and for the land we are called to heal.

He makes the storm a calm, so that its waves are still.

Psalm 120:9 WEB

Prayer:

Father God, I believe that You are the great invisible healer and Jesus is Your visible earthly messenger. Father, heal my unbelief. I believe that You can and do heal but so often I ask for Your healing touch and — apparently — nothing happens. Convict me in the deepest parts of my spirit, mind and body, that You know better than I do and if You have not answered it is because You have better plans for me and know more than I do. Help me, Father, to accept without complaint, just as Paul accepted his 'thorn in the flesh', that You know that which is best for me.

Heavenly Father, when Jesus was asked for a miracle, His reply was basically this: 'You ask for a miracle so that you will have faith and believe. You say that, if I perform a miracle, you will believe. But, My friends, that's not how the spiritual life works. You have it back to front. Once you do believe you will see evidence and signs of miracles everywhere. I cannot do anything unless the Father — your Father and Mine — wills it. Take joy in the exquisite timing when, perhaps after three decades of tearful prayer, everything finally comes together.'

Miracles are all around us. Father, You and Jesus are one. Jesus does nothing except as He sees You do.

Father God, unite my heart to revere Your name. Heal the unbelieving parts of my heart and knit them together with the believing parts. Your word says that a three-fold cord is hard to break. Father, please be that third cord I so badly need to be able to accept You unconditionally. Give me a heart to love and accept, eyes to see, ears to hear, an intellect to understand and accept all that You do and say and are.

Father, there are many times in the storms of life when I have cried for Your help. Help, Father God, help. I need help that none but You can give. I am weathering the storm of a broken relationship and I can't do it on my own. It is too painful. Come, Jesus, come — come in just the way I need You to come to touch my heart, my soul and my spirit at the deepest level. I am broken at the very core of my being and You came to heal the broken hearted — come, Lord Jesus, come and melt the pain away.

Yahweh, encircle me with the love of Jesus Christ. Cover, hide and protect me and wrap me in Your mantle of protection so I am hidden from the enemy. Hover over me and draw forth Jesus in my life in new and wonderful ways for Your glory and the healing of Your people and land.

Thank You, Father God. Thank You, Lord Jesus, and thank You, Holy Spirit. Thank You for Your 24/7 covering, protection and healing. I believe with everything in me — help my unbelief.

Amen

Discussion Questions:

(1) In what ways does Jesus show He has greater authority than the Roman emperors in this series of episodes?

(2) How are the actions and attitudes of Jesus different from those of Julius Caesar in a similar storm?

(3) How does Jesus begin, in this incident, to give hints that the 'sign of the prophet Jonah' is going to be so significant in His later ministry?

(4) What do you understand by 'authority' when it comes to dealing with demonic entities? How do you take account of Jude 1:8–10, 2 Peter 2:10–11 along with Luke 10:19–20?

(5) How are you, today, called to help still the storm in the lives of others? How are you, today, called to help others who are oppressed and in 'chains'?

They put up stone pillars to gods
and Asherah idols on every high hill
and under every green tree.

— 2 Kings 17:10 NCV —

— John 6:19 TPT —

They caught sight of Jesus
walking on top of the waves, coming toward them.
The disciples panicked.

In Small Letters

A narrative retelling of the reclaiming of three divine titles told from the perspective of the apostle Andrew.

As the crowd surged up the hillside, Andrew sighed. So much for getting away from it all. So much for a quiet morning of teaching without distraction. So much for a time of uninterrupted preparation for the Passover. *My friends, let us kiss goodbye to all that.*

With the feast so close, he'd been looking forward to a rest. He wanted to quiz Jesus about some of His stories. And perhaps that would lead to another mind-stretching parable or two. Being Passover, that might be about a householder painting the blood of a lamb on a doorpost or a wife searching for an elusive last speck of leaven. There'd be a sting in the tale, of course, but it was the unexpected elements that made His stories so memorable.

Apparently the relaxing day was not to be. *Can we slip away? Find another secluded spot?*

Andrew sighed again when it became obvious Jesus wasn't trying to get away. He seemed intent on allowing the multitude to reach them. And, no exaggeration, it *was* a multitude. *Thousands! Maybe ten thousand, if you count the women and children.*

Jesus nudged Philip. 'Where shall we buy bread for these people to eat?'

Philip seemed taken aback by the incongruity of the question.

Andrew was puzzled too. *Does He want us to head back across the lake to Capernaum? Or to trek up to Bethsaida? Or... is it a loaded question? You never can tell with Jesus.*

'Miracles are a retelling in small letters of the very same story which is written across the whole world in letters too large for some of us to see.'

CS Lewis, 'Miracles',
God in the Dock

Andrew was still waiting to hear Philip's answer when he caught sight of a boy coming from the far side of the hill. *A lost ṭāle.* The boy clutched a small patched sack as he scanned the oncoming crowd with a worried frown.

Andrew could tell anxiety when he saw it. He went to intercept the boy. 'Shalom, *ṭāle*. Can I help you?'

'My brothers...' The boy held out the sack for Andrew's inspection. 'They forgot their lunch.'

Five barley loaves. Andrew sniffed. *Two very pungent dried fish.*

He was about to comment when Philip's voice echoed across to him. 'I think we'd need about a year's wages,' Philip was telling Jesus. 'That'd buy us enough bread for each of them to have just a single bite.'

Oh, wrong answer, my friend. Andrew knew it at once. He'd been with Jesus from the first. From the moment John the Baptist had said: 'Behold, the *ṭāle* of Yahweh who takes away the sins of the world.' He'd been there too at the first miracle when Jesus had succumbed to His mother's compassion for others. He'd learned from Mary's example: *you give Jesus the necessary raw material and you give Him a challenge. With total confidence He'll come through. And the utmost courtesy, of course.*

Andrew winked at the boy. 'This young boy here has five loaves and two fish.' He had the strongest feeling that this *ṭāle* bringing lunch for his brothers was just like another boy of long ago — David the giant-killer, who'd walked into the pages of history simply because he too was bringing lunch for his brothers. 'But what good is that with this huge crowd?'

Jesus stared at him. A long moment stretched into an awkward silence. Andrew felt his soul laid bare as it dawned on him just what he'd done. Everyone called Simon the impulsive one, but Andrew knew he was just as bad. It was a family trait. *Uh...oh. I tried to manipulate the Messiah. I'm so sorry. And the boy... I didn't consider.*

'Tell everyone to sit down.' Jesus' smile was warm and forgiving as He took the bread. Giving thanks and blessing it, He broke it. And broke and broke and broke...

Hebrew Glossary

ṭāle: lamb, also *young man*

shalom: peace, also *wholeness, health, welfare, soundness; a greeting — 'peace be to you.'*

Philip was stupefied. Simon's eyes were growing more and more round by the second. Andrew shook his head, sure his sight was deceiving him.

Jesus was still giving thanks and blessing and breaking, blessing and breaking, blessing and breaking...

James and John had enough sense to run down to their boat and grab some fishing baskets. They rushed back up the hillside, flinging the baskets at anyone close enough to gather the multiplying mounds of bread.

Then Jesus started on the fish. Just as before: giving thanks, blessing, breaking. Breaking. Breaking. Breaking. Breaking...

Words were spinning around in Andrew's mind as he took up a basket, full to overflowing, and passed it around the rear of the crowd. *Dag, dagan, dagah* — fish, barley, multiplication.

Was Jesus playing with words? With the very stuff of creation? Everywhere Andrew looked men, women and children were eating with satisfaction. No one had to hold back. *Dag, dagan, dagah* — fish, barley, multiplication.

What did the sign mean? *Dag, dagan, dagah* — fish, barley, multiplication.

People were whispering. Those towards the front had seen what had happened as it happened. They'd seen the loaves, the fish... how five and two had multiplied beyond measure as Jesus gave thanks and blessed and broke. *Dag, dagan, dagah.*

'Gather up the leftover fragments,' Jesus said. 'Let nothing be wasted.'

Andrew took the opportunity to sidle up to Him. 'Everyone is saying you're the Prophet who is to come. Are You ready to be proclaimed king?'

Jesus said nothing. Just nodded.

Andrew turned to hand his basket to Simon. When he turned back a moment later, Jesus was gone.

So, he noticed, was the *ṭāle*.

Hebrew Glossary

dag: fish

dagan: barley

dagah: multiplication

The photograph opposite is, in fact, on the far side of the lake to the location of the miracle of the loaves and fishes. Jesus gave His famous sermon on the Beatitudes on one of these level-topped mountains. There is no conflict between the description of it as a 'level place' in Luke 6:17 and a mountain in Matthew 5:1.

By nightfall, Jesus still hadn't come back. *Hardly unusual.* He often went off into lonely places to pray.

Andrew's mind was still reeling. The triplet of words — *dag, dagan, dagah* — shifted and spun through his thoughts as he tried to unravel the riddle of the sign.

The Lord God created the heavens and the earth through His spoken word — so why couldn't the Son of God create likewise? After all, He's said often enough He only does what He sees the Father doing. And, as one season passes to the next, the Father multiplies each seed sown in the fields a hundredfold. Each ear of wheat comes from a single grain that sprouts and ripens into sheaves ready for harvest. It's not the multiplying that's so unusual, it's the time taken. A single season compressed into seconds.

Matthew tapped him on the shoulder, stirring him from his reverie. 'We're going, Andrew. Light's fading and your brother's a bit anxious. There's a storm coming. He wants us back in Capernaum before it hits.'

Anxious. *Daag.* Another word related to *dag, dagan, dagah.* The collection was growing. Grow. That's *dagah* too. Maybe add in *dagar*, gather, because we did a fair bit of gathering for those twelve baskets of leftovers. Did I miss a *dagal*, banner, at some point? Or could this somehow be about Dagon, the fish-and-grain godling of the ancient Philistines in the old, old story about the Ark of the Covenant?

Andrew looked around in the bright moonlight. The crowd hadn't dispersed. They were clearly waiting for Jesus to return. 'Aren't we going to wait for the rabbi?' he asked Matthew.

'Jesus is likely at Bethsaida by now.'

True enough. Andrew followed Matthew down the hillside. Even that simple action suddenly struck him as unusual. He was used to being followed, rather than following. Followed, in fact, as he introduced people to Jesus. He'd started his discipleship by taking Simon to Jesus and he found he just kept on doing the same sort of thing. Even today, with the *ṭāle.*

He clambered into the boat. The strange silence suited him. Perhaps the others were mulling over the same set of words: *dag, dagan, dagah, daag, dagal, dagar... Was it a series of seven — pointing to*

Hebrew Glossary

daag: anxious

dagar: gather

dagal: banner

the last, Dagon? But, if this was about the fish-and-grain godling, why now?

Andrew turned over the story of Dagon in his mind. There wasn't much known. The Ark of the Covenant had been lost for a time during the period of the Judges — all because of the corruption of the sons of the high priest Eli. The Philistines had captured the Ark during battle and had triumphantly placed it in the temple of their godling Dagon. In the morning, the statue of Dagon had fallen down, flat on its face, in front of the Ark. The priests had set it upright but, next day, it had not only fallen again, it was broken into several pieces on the threshold. *Broken in pieces. Threshold.*

Fish and grain. Broken in pieces. That's exactly what happened today. On the verge of the Passover: the feast of the threshold covenant. Andrew palmed his forehead. Of course! *Passover: the time that leaven must be removed from the house.*

Leaven symbolises corruption. *And anything to do with the godling Dagon is ultimately about the corruption of the high priest and his family. That's the message!*

Andrew beamed, sure he'd solved the riddle. Then he frowned. *Why would Jesus be so subtle about that? Everyone knows Annas and Caiaphas are as corrupt as it's humanly possible to be.*

A flurry of wind brought his attention back to the boat. He looked up. Look, *dagal*. Up, *dagal*. He blinked, trying to corral his unruly thoughts. Wild tatters of green-black cloud scudded across an almost-full moon.

The storm was coming far faster than Simon had anticipated. And, coming from the west, it was against them. Andrew went to help John, already straining at the oar. They pulled, in strong concerted effort, the relentless wind pushing them back. Waves crashed over the sides of the boat. The boat slewed in the churning water and a struggle began to keep it from capsizing.

It was then that Andrew decided he was dreaming. He shook his head, trying to dash the lashing water from his eyes. *It can't be.* There was Jesus, walking on the water. He was as calm and unruffled as He would have been taking a stroll in morning sunshine. *Hallucination.*

Dagon:

A godling of the Philistines, sometimes pictured as a half-man, half-fish but which may actually be a grain deity. Dagon is mentioned in 1 Samuel 5.

Hebrew glossary:

dagal: look

dagal: up

John 6:20 WEB

It was when John cried out that Andrew realised the others could see Jesus too.

'It's a ghost,' James croaked.

'It is I,' Jesus called. 'Don't be afraid.' And coming toward them He stepped into the boat. Instantly, they were at Capernaum.

Andrew's gulp caught in his throat.

That wasn't about Dagon. That was about Asherah, the goddess of the Phoenicians: 'She Who Walks On Water'. If He's saying He's greater than Asherah, then He must be saying He's greater than Dagon. But that goes without saying.

Unless... Andrew folded his lip under his top teeth, once more lost in thought. *Unless...*

It actually doesn't go without saying. Unless He knows many of the crowd are secretly baking cakes for Asherah and covertly worshipping Dagon — and who knows what other godlings.

He paused, troubled. *Unless that's what's in my own heart too.*

Asherah:

A fertility goddess in Canaanite religion. Her cult involved Asherah poles, pillars or sacred trees. Deuteronomy 16:21 explicitly forbids worship of Asherah but it cropped up repeatedly in Israelite history.

'I am the living Bread that comes down from Heaven.'

What's He doing? Andrew was stunned at how much provocation could be packed into just a few words. *True enough, if He told the crowd to go away, they'd simply ignore Him. Willing or not, He's the king they want.*

A large section of the multitude who'd been fed the previous day had tracked them down. They'd begun asking probing questions. But Jesus was obviously in no mood to be manipulated or controlled. He flung back an accusation: 'You are looking for Me, not because you saw the signs I performed but because you ate the loaves and had your fill.' And topped it with a challenge: 'Do not work for food that spoils, but for food that endures to eternal life, which the Son of Man will give you.'

He withdrew... in a boat to a deserted place, apart.

Matthew 14:13 WEB

The insults started: 'What sign then will You give that we may see it and believe You? What will You do?'

Like, what? Andrew was incredulous. *What sign? Didn't they hear Him?* You're looking for Me, not because you saw the signs... *Wasn't the bread enough? Wasn't the fish enough? Wasn't the sevenfold dag, dagan, dagah, daag, dagal, dagar overcoming of Dagon enough?*

'Our ancestors ate the manna in the wilderness,' one of the crowd's spokesmen went on. 'As it is written: He gave them bread from heaven to eat.'

'Very truly I tell you, it is not Moses who has given you the bread from heaven, but it is My Father who gives you the true bread from heaven.'

Andrew was startled. The answer was simple enough. But it tore straight through the ambiguity of the spokeman's pious response. *How had Jesus discerned that this man actually believed Moses*

had been the bread-giver? Andrew glanced around and realised, with an even greater shock, that the idea was not uncommon. He was appalled.

Moses, the messiah of old, has been elevated to a godling in some people's thinking — and here, to their minds, is the new Messiah. So that means to them that not only is our deliverance from the Romans at hand but that 'Moses' the bread-giver is back again. He shook his head at the incongruity of the thought: Jesus, dispensing daily manna, not from the desert but from downtown Capernaum by the fish-docks.

Not going to happen, folks.

It was beginning to make sense. Andrew had been puzzled that Jesus was willing enough to let the Samaritans proclaim Him as the Messiah, but not His own people. The Samaritans had relatively few pre-conceived notions about the Messiah, so Jesus could be Himself. But the Jews, no. The strength of their wrong ideas about the Messiah might just be enough to propel Jesus to a place He didn't want to go.

The ruthless side of Jesus was coming out. He was intent, like the most diligent of wives before the Passover, on scouring the house clean of every last bit of leaven. The last spot of corrupted, infected thinking had to be thrown out.

'I am the bread of life.'

Huh? Oh no. Andrew was perplexed. *Why get rid of the leavened thinking only to introduce this?* He thought back to the previous day: to the assault on Dagon. That was subtle, unobtrusive. *But this, no. No one's going to miss the reference to Asherah's consort. You can't say, 'I am the Bread of Life' and expect people will not know You're referring to Tammuz.*

And then he realised. The same consistent, unswerving message had been threaded throughout the last twenty-four hours: that God has sent the Son and He is greater than the Chaldean harvest godling, Tammuz. He is greater than Asherah, the walker-on-water. He is greater than Dagon of the Philistines.

Andrew heard the murmuring of the crowd, the quiet horror that Jesus had used the name of Yahweh in reference to Himself, while

Tammuz:

A Chaldean harvest godling and consort of Ishtar, the Babylonian equivalent of Asherah. Tammuz is mentioned in Ezekiel 8:14.

claiming a title of Tammuz. The grumbling intensified. There might be secret worshippers of Asherah here — people who, in defiance of the Pharisees, had a bit of a bet on the side when it came to divine protection. There might be those who had a hidden place where they did some wailing for Tammuz at the appropriate season — but these were things everyone knew never to bring out into the open. Jesus was threatening their hearts — and they couldn't hear what He was really saying.

They couldn't see that Tammuz had usurped the titles, 'Bread of Life' and 'Bread that comes down from heaven' They couldn't grasp that 'She Who Walks On Water' is a stolen designation that rightly belongs to the Father. They couldn't take in that it wasn't the heroism of Moses that brought manna from heaven but the grace of God.

And they couldn't see that Jesus was taking those titles back.

Andrew watched, in disbelief, as many of Jesus' disciples turned their backs and simply walked away, along with a rapidly dispersing crowd.

He heard Jesus ask the twelve closest to Him: 'You do not want to leave too, do you?'

Thank God the Father for impulsive Simon. Andrew nodded vigorously as he heard his brother say: 'Lord, to whom shall we go? You have the words of eternal life. We have come to believe and to know that you are the Holy One of God.'

Comments:

CS Lewis wrote, 'Miracles are a retelling in small letters of the very same story which is written across the whole world in letters too large for some of us to see.'

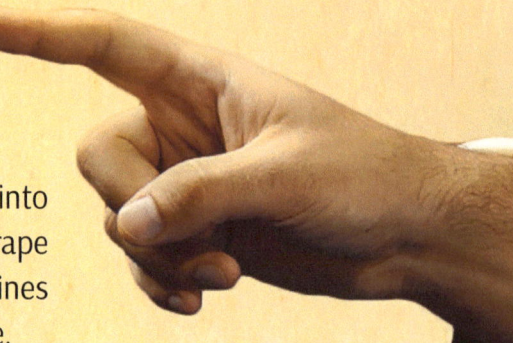

When Jesus performed His first miracle at Cana, turning water into wine, He followed the example of His Father. Every day, along grape vines, a miracle of the Father's creation unfolds as water combines with light and trace minerals to become clusters of fruit for wine.

The miracle of the loaves and fishes also adheres to this pattern. Jesus does what He sees the Father doing. (John 5:19) Just as fish multiply in the sea, just as grain sprouts and multiplies on the ear, this miracle reminds us of the creative provision of the Father for our daily needs.

This imaging of God's way points up the critical difference between magic and miracle. When the satan tempted Jesus to command stones to become bread (Matthew 4:3), he was asking for a demonstration of power against the natural order. God created plants to yield seed after their own kind and animals to bear young after their own kind. To use His divine creative energy to transgress these boundaries is to cross over into occult activity: since, in essence, magic is simply the use of God's creative principles of design and power against Him and His ordained order.

Now, some commentators believe that this incident has a more commonplace explanation. They consider that, when the crowd saw the little boy offer up his lunch of loaves and fish, they quietly took out their own supplies and handed them around their neighbours. Now, admittedly such unselfish sharing would indeed be a miracle of a very high order! However I don't think the gospel writer intended us to have that understanding as even a remote option.

The narrative John presents to us in the sixth chapter of his gospel has, first of all, five thousand men being fed by Jesus (not counting the women and children). Before Jesus explains that 'He is the Bread Come Down From Heaven' — an event which occurs on the next day and which led to a huge loss in His following — He walks on water. All too often we see this as an entirely separate incident, instead of integral to the story of this miracle. But once we realise this is a declaration of war against the goddess Asherah, we can hardly fail to recognise a similar attack on Tammuz and Dagon.

This was just an opening salvo: Jesus was soon to bring the war right into the heart of pagan territory. In addition, He constantly reclaimed the titles of the gods of the nations for His Father — each of His 'I AM' statements is an assertion that His Father is the rightful owner of designations like *The Light of the World*, *The True Vine*, *The Good Shepherd* and *The Gate of the Sheep* that were claimed by the godlings Mithras, Dionysius, Pan and Janus respectively.

Don't work for the food which perishes, but for the food which remains...

This apparent fusion of the sacred name of God — 'I AM' — with Jesus' own identity as well as a title of a foreign godling was too great a leap of understanding for the majority of His followers. They didn't see that Jesus was claiming back these epithets; they saw a call for syncretic worship, forbidden by the Torah.

The timing of Jesus' miracle is significant. It was close to the Passover and thus to the seven-day Feast of Unleavened Bread. This festival commemorated the time when the people of Israel, enslaved to the Egyptians, were liberated by God. He had commanded them to leave swiftly — not even allowing their bread to rise.

Ancient peoples used to gather yeast from grape leaves to leaven their bread and make the dough rise. But God had told the Israelites to go in haste — and to ever after remember their first taste of freedom with the week-long Festival of Unleavened Bread. And to do that, they had to get all yeast out of the house — not an easy task, given that yeast from grape leaves was airborne and could float in any time.

God tells us 'yeast' represents *sin*. So the attempt to eradicate yeast in the house for a week represents our commitment to removing sin from our lives. And so when Jesus claimed to be the 'Bread of Life', 'The Bread Come Down From Heaven', at the season of the Passover, He meant us to understand He is the Unleavened Bread, the bread without yeast, the food without sin.

And what was that bit about eating Him that so upset His followers? To eat food dedicated to a deity was to 'become one' with that idol. Even today we know 'you are what you eat'. The term 'delicacies' originated in food ritually offered in a temple sacrifice and later consumed by the worshippers.

The first Council of Jerusalem, while deciding Gentiles did not need to be circumcised to become Christians, nonetheless required that they refrain from food offered to idols as well as sexual immorality — in other words, from activities that would make them covenantally one with those opposed to God.

Instead, they were to maintain *'one Lord, one faith, one baptism, one God and Father of all who is over all and through all and in all.'* (Ephesians 4:5 NAS)

"Loaves and Fishes"

Prayer:

Thank You, Father God, for the freedom You have given us through Jesus.

Thank You, Father God, for the daily bread You have given us through Jesus.

Thank You, Father God, for the spiritual food You have given us through Jesus.

Thank You, Father God, for the covenant You have given us through Jesus.

Thank You, Father God, for the salvation You have given us through Jesus.

Thank You, Father God, for the healing You have given us through Jesus.

Thank You, Father God, for the example of miraculous works You have given us through Jesus.

Thank You, Father God, for the reminders of Your everyday creative power You have given us through Jesus.

Thank You, Father God, for the cleansing of heart and mind You have given us through Jesus.

Thank You, Father God, for the conviction of sin You have given us through Your Spirit.

Thank You, Father God, for the redemption of names You have given us through Jesus.

Teach us to follow Him, to acknowledge and believe He is the Holy One of God and, as He told us, to do even greater works than He did.

In His name and through the power of His cross.

Amen

Discussion Questions:

(1) What do you understand by 'covenant'? Does it include an aspect of oneness?

(2) What happens to our relationship with God when we covenant with anyone opposed to Him?

(3) Buy some matzah bread — bread for the Passover that is striped, pierced, unleavened and made in less than 18 minutes (the amount of time that it takes for cut grain to begin fermenting after it is exposed to moisture). What symbolism is represented by the

    (a) striping
    (b) piercing
    (c) lack of yeast
    (d) rapid baking

(4) While it is notoriously difficult to spot the 'leavening' in our own lives or worldview since it infiltrates the whole of our thinking, is there any problematic speck the Lord has pointed out to you that He wants removed? Why are you ignoring it?

(5) What are the 'hard sayings' of Jesus that tempt you to turn away from following Him?

Glory be to God for dappled things —
    For skies of couple-colour as a brinded cow;
      For rose-moles all in stipple upon trout that swim;
Fresh-firecoal chestnut-falls; finches' wings;
    Landscape plotted and pieced — fold, fallow, and plough;
      And áll trádes, their gear and tackle and trim.

All things counter, original, spare, strange;
    Whatever is fickle, freckled (who knows how?)
      With swift, slow; sweet, sour; adazzle, dim;
He fathers-forth whose beauty is past change:
        Praise him.

                Gerard Manley Hopkins

Afterword

many-coloured: *poikilos*

This word is used by the apostle Peter to describe *grace*. With overtones of variegated, diverse, kaleidoscopic, rainbow-hued, assorted and manifold, it conveys the richness and range of this power coming from God's Spirit.

Poikilos aptly describes the diversity of ways Jesus healed history. At one moment His actions were small, private and hidden, at others they were bold, public and dramatic. Consider the contrast between the meeting with the woman at the well and the stilling of the storm on the lake. The first was quiet and unobtrusive, calling back the heart of Samaria to the true king; the second was a spectacular confrontation with the spiritual powers as well as the Caesars.

Yet this very diversity should encourage us. Perhaps we're not ready to turn the tide of battle against the principalities in our own sphere of influence; but even as toddlers, we learned to ask for a drink. And that's all it took to begin the healing of Shechem.

So whatever your stage of faith, be inspired by the actions of Jesus — and whether He's calling you to the secretive and simple or to the audacious and breath-taking, hear His whisper: 'Courage, dear heart!' and follow Him.

Acknowledgments & Attributions

Photo and Arts Credits

Cover — rayeq-dowery/istockphoto | Description: Lupinus at Nazareth in Israel
Liana Mikah/Unsplash | Description: field of wildflowers

Page 7 — aldra/istockphoto | Description: Young woman wrapped in oranged shawl scarf

Page 8 — Ayman Ameen/APA Images/ZUMA Wire/Alamy Live News | Description: Members of the Samaritan sect take part in a traditional pilgrimage marking the holiday of Passover atop Mount Gerizim near the West Bank city of Nablus on 17 April 2017. The Samaritans practice a religion that is based on four principles of faith, one God —— the God of Israel; one Prophet —— Moses Ben Amram; the belief in the Torah —— the first five books of the Bible and one holy place —— Mount Gerizim

Page 10 — naeblys/istockphoto | Description: Map of Israel, map and borders, hand drawn, reliefs and lakes

Page 13 — nopow/istockphoto | Description: Woman in the Middle East

Page 14 — Photo Credit: Shadi Jarar'Ah/APA Images/ZUMA Wire/Alamy Live News | Description: Samaritan worshippers pray on the top of Mount Gerizim in a traditional pilgrimage to mark Shavuot at dawn near the West Bank city of Nablus on 24 June 2018. Shavuot commemorates the giving of the Torah at Mount Sinai seven weeks after the exodus of the Jewish people from Egypt.

Page 15 — Joel Carillet/istockphoto | Description: Landscape with olive trees in Nablus

Page 16 — LycheeStudio/canstockphoto | Description: Red Anemones Field Winter Blooming Macro Shot in Green Grass Field, Beeri Forest, Southern District of Israel

Page 20 — Sojourner87/istockphoto | Description: Mountain Gerizim and Ebal in Israel

Page 21 — Genevieve Arthy | Description: 'The Woman at the Well'

Page 23 — Jacek_Sopotnicki/istockphoto | Description: Sea of Galilee from eastern shore

Page 24 — standby/istockphoto | Description: 'Into The Heat of Battle'

Page 26 — naeblys/istockphoto | Description: Map of Israel, map and borders, hand drawn, reliefs and lakes;
lagui/istockphoto | Description: Roman legionary

Page 29 — ginosphotos/istockphoto | Description: Jesus and Roman centurion

Page 30 — zepperwing/istockphoto | Description: Kursi ruin, a monastery built on the traditional site of the healing of the two demonic men

Page 33 — thawornnurak/istockphoto | Description: Grunge rustic chain;
SerhiiBobyk /istockphoto | Description: Young warrior on a mountain peak

Page 35 — sakcpaint/istockphoto | Description: silhouette pig in sunset

Page 36-7— FXQuadro/istockphoto | Description: Complete combat equipment of the ancient Greek warrior lie on a box of wooden boards

Page 39 — Genevieve Arthy | Description: 'From Darkness to Light'

Page 40 — makarenko07/istockphoto | Description: Evening storm on the Sea of Galilee

Page 43 — Irisangel/CanStockPhoto | Description: Calla Lilies on Black

Page 45 — Fred Froese/istockphoto | Description: Sea of Galilee

Page 46 — javax/istockphoto | Description: Israeli Landscape near Kinneret Lake (Sea of Galilee)

Page 48 — naeblys /istockphoto | Description: Map of Israel, map and borders, hand drawn, reliefs and lakes

Page 51 — tsafreer /istockphoto | Description: Mount Arbel Cliff Cave Fortress

Page 52 — svarshik/istockphoto | Description: Sunset on Lake Kinneret near the town of Tiberias

Page 54-55 — KristiLinton/istockphoto | Description: Walking on water

Page 57 — RnDmS/istockphoto | Description: Nachal (stream) Samach and the Golan Heights

Page 64 — Genevieve Arthy | Description: 'Loaves and Fishes'

Page 66–67 — vrihu/CanStockPhoto | Description: Pennywort

Design, including endpapers and floral iconography: Beckon Creative | beckoncreative.biz

Prayers: Dell Hamilton

Bible Versions

Scripture quotations used in colour (red or purple) throughout the text are taken from the Holy Bible, New International Version®, NIV®. Copyright © 1973, 1978, 1984, 2011 by Biblica, Inc.™ Used by permission of Zondervan. All rights reserved worldwide. www.zondervan.com The "NIV" and "New International Version" are trademarks registered in the United States Patent and Trademark Office by Biblica, Inc™.

Scripture quotations marked BSB are taken from the The Holy Bible, Berean Study Bible, BSB Copyright ©2016 by Bible Hub Used by Permission. All Rights Reserved Worldwide.

Scripture quotations marked ESV are taken from the ESV® Bible (The Holy Bible, English Standard Version®), copyright © 2001 by Crossway, a publishing ministry of Good News Publishers. Used by permission. All rights reserved.

Scripture quotations marked GNT are from the Good News Translation in Today's English Version- Second Edition Copyright © 1992 by American Bible Society. Used by Permission.

Scripture quotations marked NCV are taken from the New Century Version®. Copyright © 2005 by Thomas Nelson. Used by permission. All rights reserved.

Scripture quotations marked NLT are taken from the Holy Bible, New Living Translation, copyright 1996, 2004. Used by permission of Tyndale House Publishers, Inc., Wheaton, Illinois 60189. All rights reserved.

Scripture quotations marked TPT are from The Passion Translation®. Copyright © 2017, 2018 by Passion & Fire Ministries, Inc. Used by permission. All rights reserved. ThePassionTranslation.com.

Scripture quotations marked WEB are from the World English Bible, a modern translation of the American Standard Version.Public Domain.

Endpaper poems

Wildpeace from *Selected Poetry*, copyright © 1996 Yehuda Amichai. Reprinted by permission of University of California Press
Pied Beauty from *Pied beauty : a selection of poems.* Gerard Manley Hopkins, 1844–1889.

© Anne Hamilton 2019

Published by Armour Books

P. O. Box 492, Corinda QLD 4075 AUSTRALIA

ISBN: 978-1-925380-17-0

A catalogue record for this book is available from the National Library of Australia

All rights reserved. No part of this publication may be reproduced, stored in, or introduced into a retrieval system, or transmitted, in any form, or by any means (electronic, mechanical, photocopying, recording or otherwise) without the prior written permission of the publisher.

www.ingramcontent.com/pod-product-compliance
Lightning Source LLC
Chambersburg PA
CBHW041354100526
44816CB00045B/46